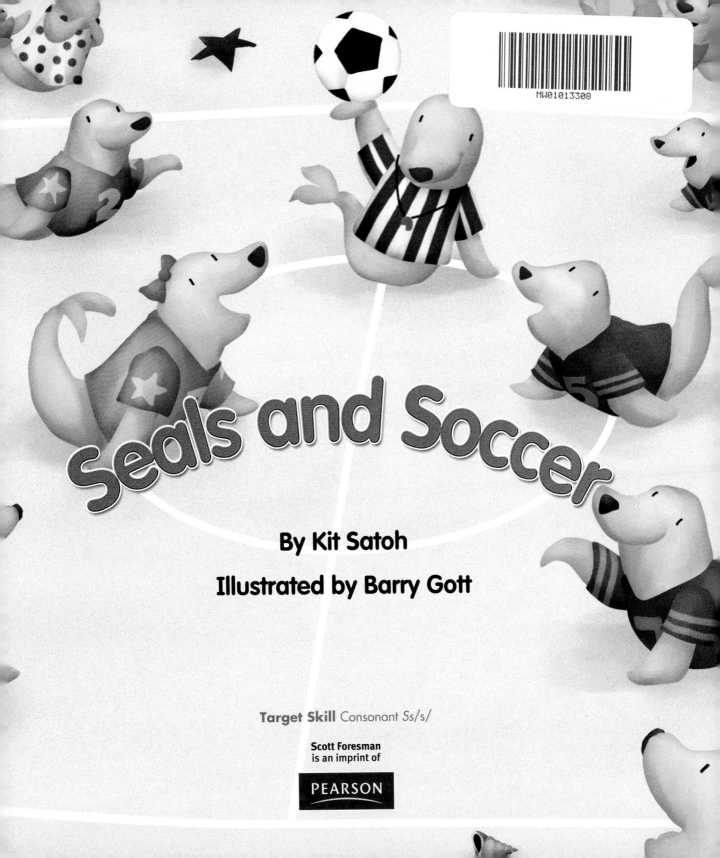

Seals and Soccer

By Kit Satoh

Illustrated by Barry Gott

Target Skill Consonant Ss/s/

Scott Foresman
is an imprint of

PEARSON

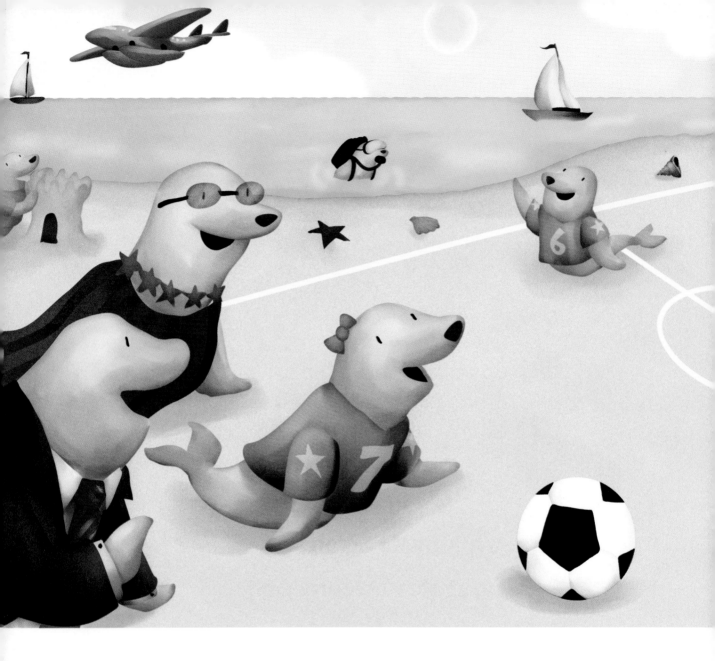

Sam

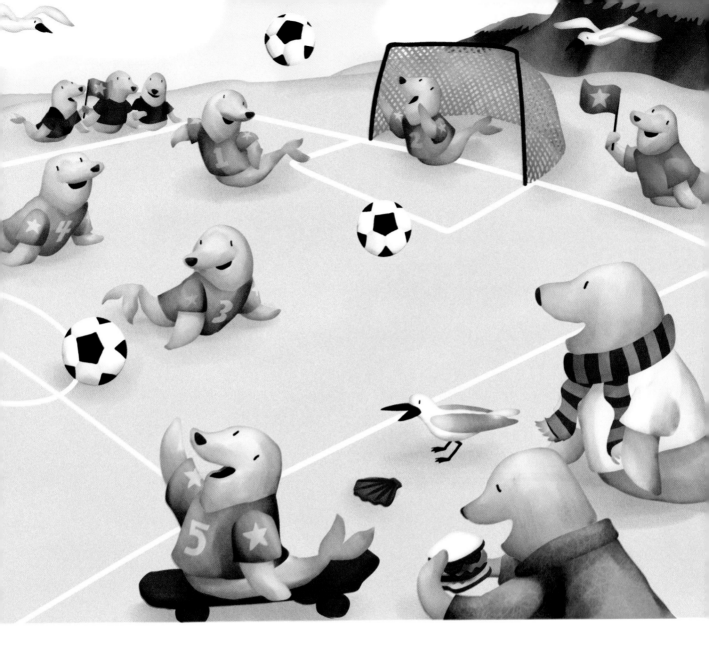

I am Sam.

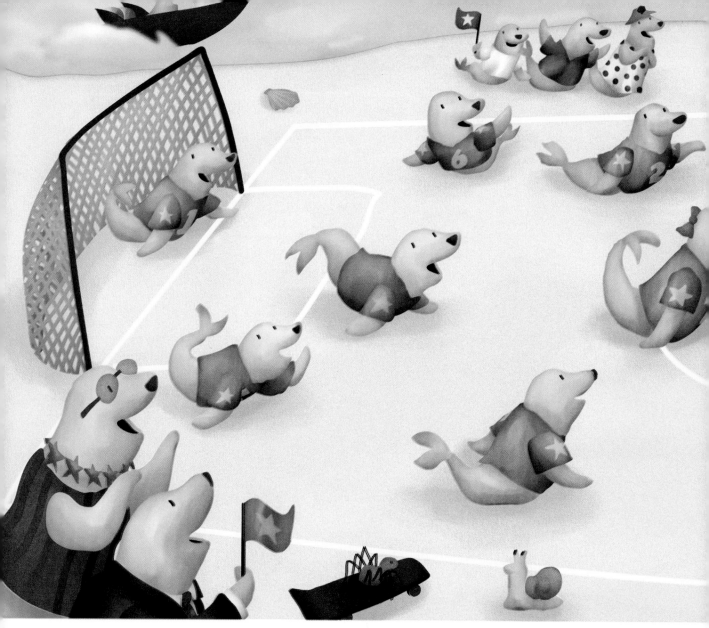

seal

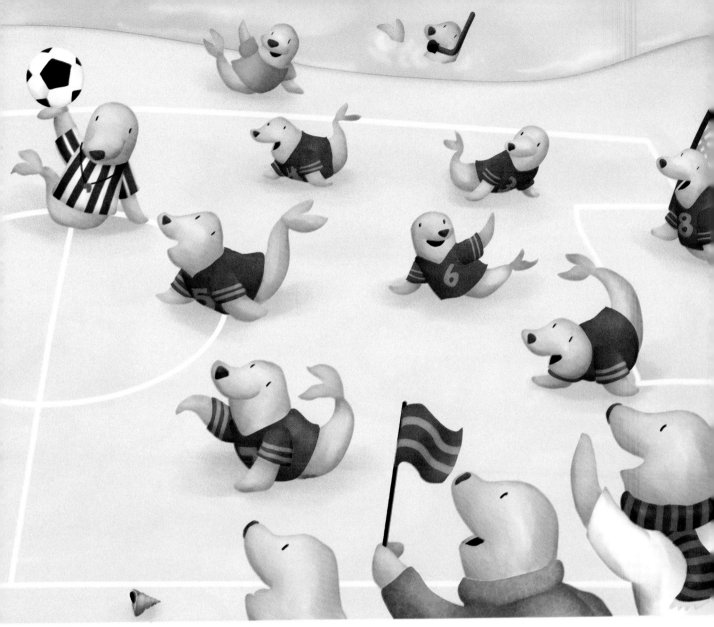

I am a seal.

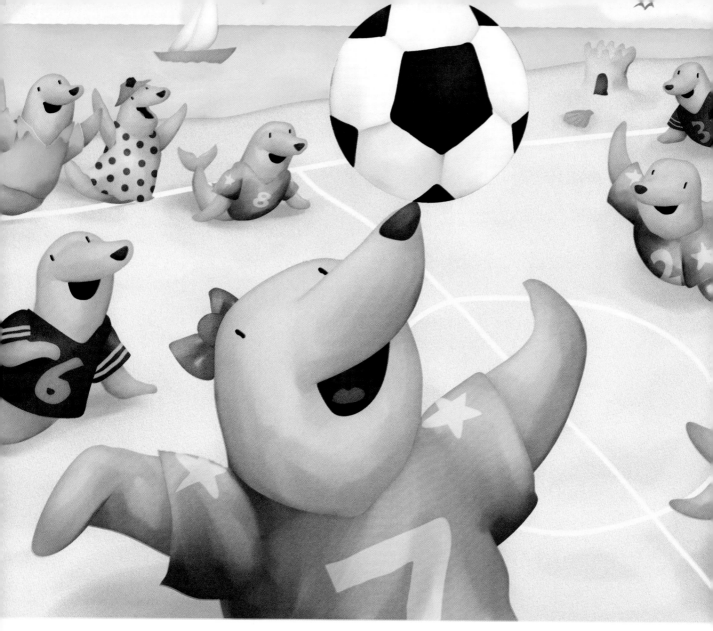

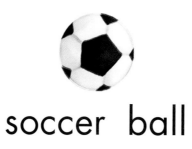

soccer ball

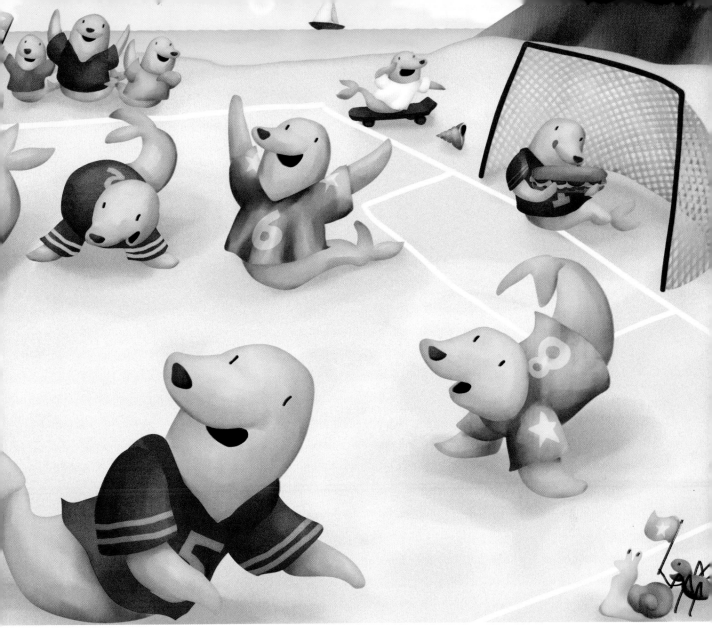

I have the soccer ball.

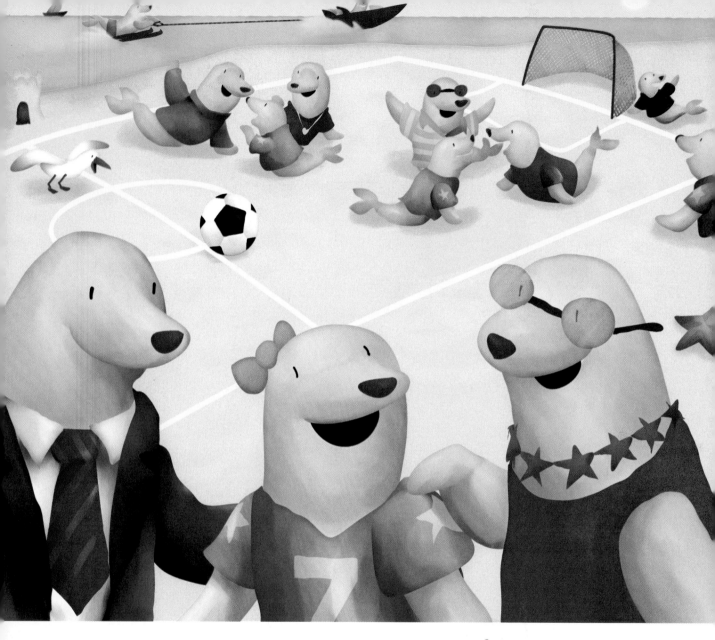

I am Sam the seal.